BRITISH RAILWAYS IN COLOUR No.2

A
British Railways
IIllustrated Special

Copyright IRWELL PRESS Ltd.,
ISBN 1-903266-05-X
First published in the
United Kingdom in 2001
by Irwell Press Ltd.,
59A, High Street, Clophill,
Bedfordshire MK45 4BE
Printed by The Amadeus Press

Few sights quite evoked the air of an earlier age (an earlier century more like) than the Stroudley 0-6-0 tanks. They were famous survivors and quite a few have found their way into preservation including No.32640. The engine started out life in 1878 as A1 class No.40 BRIGHTON. The locos were built for the South and East London lines and No.40 won a prize for the LB&SCR at the Paris Exhibition in 1878. The engine was sold off to the Isle of Wight Central in 1902 which became part of the Southern Railway in 1923. The engine went back to the mainland in 1947 and became 32640 in 1951. Incredibly, it lasted for more than another decade and was not withdrawn by BR until 1963. After a period on static display at Butlins Pwllheli from 1964 until 1973 the engine returned to the Isle of Wight where it can still be seen today at Haven Street. Here it is towards the end of its BR working life, at the little Hayling Island terminus on 23 August 1959.

INTRODUCTION

The steam era in Britain was one of the glories of the last two centuries. Now, fewer and fewer people remember the time when the great part of the nation's goods and passengers went by rail. The railways had quickly risen to become, effectively, the sole carrier in the British Isles, a position they held for decade after decade. It was a position that only began to be undermined after the Great War and one that was not eclipsed until the coming of car ownership, long distance roads, motorways and airlines.

The system of competing railways was essentially in place well before 1900, serving any habitation of any importance throughout the land. The primacy of the railway was fading long before the Second World War but it was not really evident until the 1950s were coming to a close. It was an era to be savoured; it was 'sooty but safe' but its workings were becoming sclerotic – a host of bureaucrats (I was one of them!) ran the nationalised British Railways from 1948 and as their offices got larger so the system got smaller. In the

early 1950s, with widespread car ownership still only a dream, the railway was a part of all of our lives. You did not really think twice about travelling by train on Christmas day for instance. It is hard to believe now that nearly everyone lived within earshot of working steam, the system running all day and night, high days and holidays. Most people were familiar with the sound of shunting, far off in the night.

Britain fairly oozed steam, smoke, soot and grit and when the mid-winter light finally percolated the gloom some ideal photographic opportunities emerged. The environment was polluted, but no one seemed particularly aware of the fact, even if many trains were grubby and engines more often than not dirty and unpolished. In the country the local branch line served the community and the railway staff enjoyed some status. 'Their' station might be cluttered up with boxes, parcels and an odd mix of goods but the station was kept clean and tidy and the garden well maintained. The signalboxes were kept spick and span with polished levers, block instruments and bright lino. The mechanical age of signalling went with steam, along with musty coaching stock and guards waving their flags and blowing whistles. The paraphernalia, such as creaking barrows, flickering oil or gas lamps and fogmen's horns were all part of the steam age 'background noise'. For most of us, beginning photography in the 1950s, 'colour' did not present itself as a real possibility in terms of cost and quality until the dawn of the 1960s, and the vast bulk of colour photography that we see today is accordingly concentrated in those last years, as steam teetered on the edge of its final fall from grace. Yet it is true that the railways often still had the air about them of a much earlier age. I hope some of the 'sooty but safe' quality of those times has crept into this collection.

C. Gammell; all photographs by the author, except where shown.

Wimbledon in September 1964, and the down Atlantic Coast Express passes with rebuilt Merchant Navy Pacific No.35022 HOLLAND AMERICA LINE. The engine has survived and awaits full restoration; it was built in 1948, rebuilt in 1956 and withdrawn from BR in 1966. Ten of Bulleid's MN class have survived in one form or another while another, No.35029 ELLERMAN LINES, is displayed in sectioned form at the National Railway Museum, York. On the right the 'glasshouse' SR signalbox operates the semaphore signals and a 4SUB unit leaves with a Waterloo stopper.

The down Bournemouth Belle passes Clapham Junction on 11 March 1967 shortly before electrification. The wheezy Merchant Navy, No.35003 ROYAL MAIL, was built in 1941, rebuilt in 1959 and lasted until July 1967. The 'air smoothed' engines raised eyebrows when introduced; after rebuilding the controversy settled down somewhat but continues in one form or another to the present day. Many claim the rebuilt engines to be far superior to the originals with their chain gear, while others insist (producing figures to demonstrate it so) that though the new engines might be effective, they were not so much better that the enormous expense of rebuilding was justified. See the recent *Book of the Merchant Navy Pacifics* (Irwell Press) for the latest developments of the arguments.

No.W33 BEMBRIDGE charges out of Ryde Esplanade on 26 June 1960, the little O2 0-4-4T leading a ramshackle train of LBSCR and SECR stock. The service provided by the SR was eminently reasonable for what was really a collection of remote branches depending on internal connections like no others. The Southern upgraded much of the lines, the buildings and the stock after 1923 and though they might look ancient, the trains did a sterling job of moving thousands of families and their luggage every summer Saturday from Cowes and Ryde, inland to their digs, caravans, boarding houses and hotels.

Pannier tank ubiquity: the old Brecon & Merthyr/LNWR joint line from Merthyr in November 1961 with No.6416 at Pontsarn, with a Merthyr to Pontsticill stopping passenger train. The 6400 class was a version of the 57XXs intended mainly for passenger work and dating from 1932 – they were push-pull fitted. The 'B&M' traversed some fine mountain scenery and stiff gradients such as the four miles at 1 in 40 to Pantywaun Junction on the B&M main line. Regrettably the Merthyr to Pontsticill Junction line closed on 13 November 1961, a few days after this photograph was taken.

N class 2-6-0 No.31411 propels the weedkilling train down the reversible track at East Croydon in April 1965 – the cranes rearing up point to the monstrous rebuilding taking place. The train consists of a Maunsell coach, leading a collection of old tenders from scrapped engines. The ensemble went on tour around the Region in the spring months and covered every line. The chemicals were so strong that nothing grew on the track for over a year; this was a truly 'scorched earth' (or 'scorched ballast') approach and today there is a less severe regime, doubtless due to different health and safety and environmental considerations.

A tired and dirty BR Standard class 5 4-6-0 whisks a hefty load of Gresley bogie vans through East Croydon in July 1964. This is a Newcastle to Hove pigeon special; No.73159 worked the train through to Hove where the eight Gresley bogies were unloaded and the contents (a 'flock' is hardly adequate) released to darken the sky. Pigeon fanciers on Tyneside waited for their birds to fly home north, the railway staff at Hove having opened all the baskets and recorded the time of release. The annual event took some considerable organising and the train became known to local railway staff (for reasons not difficult to work out) as the *Squitters Express*. After coal and water at nearby Brighton shed the 4-6-0 would work the return empties.

'The English Country Branch' was personified, it could be said, by the old SER Dunton Green to Westerham line, seen here on 20 March 1960 with an all pre-Grouping train. The H class 0-4-4T 31519 (shedded at Tonbridge and built in 1909) sizzles happily in the bay platform at Dunton Green with a composite LB&SCR coach, first class compartment leading. 31519 was converted to push and pull working in July 1952 and withdrawn in February 1961. The class was popular for branch line and stopping passenger work and powerful enough for

rapid acceleration away from intermediate stops. The SR demoted ex-main line stock for branch line work as electrification schemes progressed. In the distant view the H is departing Dunton Green for Westerham with its Brighton set. The cattle in the field are quite unconcerned by the train, which passed so frequently that they got used to the noise and hiss of steam.

More 'English Country Branch'. The course of the Westerham branch has largely been buried under the M25 motorway; the scale of the destruction will be evident from this picture at Brasted for instance, where H No.31519 is leaving for the branch terminus on 20 March 1960. The line opened on 6 July 1881; the promoters wanted to join up with the rest of the system but the branch only got as far as

Westerham. BR closed the line on 30 October 1961 and though a scheme followed to run it as a preserved railway this fell through. Reaching journey's end, No.31519 later rests amid the faded glories of the old SE&CR station – gas lamps dangling down from the roof. The SR green and cream paintwork is peeling away.

The V2 2-6-2s were the Gresley main line 'mixed traffic' engines for the LNER though in performance terms they were not far short of the A3 Pacifics. Lumped (very properly) with the Pacifics this gave the East Coast an extraordinary numerical superiority over the West Coast when it came to top rank power. The V2s could be seen on the East Coast main line on express passenger work but were exceptionally valuable for fast fitted freights and van trains. They were especially effective in Scotland where curves and gradients blunted the best efforts of the Pacifics. The class was introduced in 1936 and eventually reached 184 engines, of which some were named – sometimes eccentrically, with the longest names in the country. No.60870 is on the 12.54pm stopping train on 19 February 1961 at Donington Road on the former GN&GE Joint line. The station is oil lit and in Eastern Region colours. Maroon Gresley coaches form the train which is protected by semaphore signals. Serving a very rural area of Lincolnshire, the intermediate stations on the line closed in September 1961.

Gresley A4 Pacific No 60025 FALCON rushes along the East Coast main line on 1 September 1962 with an up express near the tunnels at Hadley Wood – Potters Bar tunnel is just out of sight around the curve and the train is shortly to enter Hadley North tunnel. The grubby BR Mark 1 coaches in BR maroon were typical of the day and poorly lit at night. Many Mark 1s survive on the preserved lines and can give the passenger a good view in the open saloons but cinders soon waft in from the windows. Built as No.4484 in January 1937 the engine survived under BR until October 1963.

Jubilee No.45622 NYASALAND stops for water at High Wycombe on 25 May 1963 with excursion 1X50 for Wembley Central, a special for the Cup Final. The fans dangle out of the windows of the all maroon Mark 1s, rattles at the ready for the stormy departure. The line was joint Great Central and Great Western prior to Grouping; there is a GWR type home signal in the background together with an LMS van. The Western Region perpetuated the GWR semaphores after 1948 – notable for the lower quadrants whereas the other three of the Big Four employed upper quadrant. Note the casual way the 'bag' of the water column is draped over the pipe, no doubt to get the hideous flapping, dripping thing out of the way! Observe the gaping local, all ears and short back and sides, stretching to the limit to take in the full glory of NYASALAND.

A 4F 0-6-0 working a pick up freight on the Somerset and Dorset, at Sturminster Newton on 2 August 1960. The 4Fs were a huge class, originating as a Midland design from Derby. The freight here consists mainly of vacuum fitted stock but with a few non-vacuum wagons on the rear. The station had been the Southern's concern since responsibilities had been 'divvied up' in 1935; the nameboards are SR survivals but the platform notices with their Gill sans lettering are post-1948. The timetables on the walls are in time-honoured tabular form and the gas light broods over the scene. The S&D closed on 7 March 1966.

The traditional branch line scene, as viewed from the rear of an Upton-on-Seven to Ashchurch train on 4 July 1959. Ripple station of the former Midland Railway looks a little woebegone but the goods yard is still in use and a wagon load of coal has been delivered. On the evidence of the abandoned platform and the space under the bridge the line has been singled through here. The MR opened their through line to Malvern to compete with the GWR but BR cut it back to Upton-on-Severn in 1952. The passenger service on the section to Ashchurch ended in August 1961 and Ripple was left derelict. The station was bought after closure and has now been completely restored by Mrs Fullerlove who got the idea from Petworth in Sussex. The track has been removed but the flowerbeds and station garden are now far finer than in BR days.

Upton-on Severn on 12 August 1961, a scene to gladden any Midland heart though, sadly, this was near the end. On the last day, in August 1961, 3F 0-6-0 No.43754 rests prior to running round the two coach train from Ashchurch. The MR built an ornate red brick station and brought its own equipment – note such company features as the MR slanted fencing (which the NER and LYR, among others, also employed) and the gorgeous gas lamp to the left of the engine. The 85E shedplate denotes the old Midland shed at Gloucester, absorbed into the Western Region and termed Barnwood to distinguish it from the GWR's Horton Road shed nearby. The magnificent station building was demolished after closure and the site is now occupied by the Fire Station.

No colour book can be complete, it seems, without a grimy maroon 'Big Lizzie'. No.46238 CITY OF CARLISLE is at Carlisle Citadel on 15 April 1963, ready for the off southbound with the 3.45pm to Euston. It was an Upperby engine and by the early 1960s the 8P Pacifics were largely relegated to reliefs and stopping trains. The leading coach is of interest as it is an LMS design which was a forerunner of the BR Mark I type standard vehicle. The engine was built at Crewe in 1939 and was streamlined until 1947; it was withdrawn by BR in 1964.

At the back of Ryde shed a service coach nestles on 27 September 1959. The Southern proceeded thriftily in the island; the new engine shed, replacing a fearful hovel of a place, used redundant LBSCR electrification masts, for instance. Of LBSCR origin, No.DS70008 was the breakdown coach for the whole of the island; it was in pristine condition, having just been overhauled in the adjacent works. The coach was built in 1916 at Lancing as an invalid saloon but was sent to the IOW in 1932 under the SR regime. It lasted under BR until 1968.

No.5911 PRESTON HALL at Cardiff Canton on 17 April 1960, having enjoyed a clean up prior to its next working. The GWR/BR Brunswick green is shown to full effect – it was adopted as the BR livery for express passenger types in 1948 but the Halls did not all get green until the later part of the 1950s. From thereon Swindon Works put Brunswick green on all its more important charges. The Castles in the background are both notable – 5080 DEFIANT and 4079 PENDENNIS CASTLE.

A fascinating survival (though by this time condemned – hence the daubed X) was this LNWR coach awaiting disposal in the sidings at Olney on 16 March 1961. The fading red and cream livery, once the BR standard, was superseded in 1960 by the all maroon colour, similar to the LMS standard of pre-1948 years.

A truly ancient relic, a mobile crane in the sidings at Olney on the Bedford to Northampton branch in 1961. These could be used in country goods yards which did not have enough traffic to keep a permanent crane at work. The crane would be moved with a runner to rest the jib and there were several makers providing them for the pre-Group companies. The ironwork, jib and heavy (wheeled!) balance weight suggest a Victorian owner, possibly the LNWR. By 1961 it would have been on the road to scrapping.

Steam on the Portpatrick & Wigtownshire Joint line. BR Class 4 2-6-4T No.80061 is on a stopping passenger, trailing a mixed bag of stock near Parton on 29 May 1965. The poor old dirty tank is heading a BR Mark I coach followed by an LMS brake second, a GUV and a vacuum fitted van. The guard is looking out of the brake window of his compartment on this ideal country train. Regrettably the 'Port Road' closed soon afterwards, on 14 June 1965.

The token pick-up apparatus at Creetown, on the long run to Stranraer. Engines could pick up the token at speed, the signalman setting the road up ready for the oncoming train, with the tablet picked up by the catcher on the cabside of the locomotive. The tip is lit by the black oil lamp, with access for the signalman from the wooden step and platform. The gradient post shows how undulating was the road to Stranraer.

A view backwards from the 3.20 Inverness to Perth train on Tuesday 14 July 1959 showing the two liveries then in use. The maroon replaced the red and cream from 1956 onwards but was superseded by the final BR blue and grey all line livery, 'scientifically created' we were told. In the background the lengthy viaduct crossed the River Findhorn at 143ft. Opened in 1898 the new direct line of the Highland Railway saved considerable time as the route was 34½ miles from Inverness to Aviemore compared with the old route via Forres – twenty-five miles shorter.

Crossing trains at Tain (Ross & Cromarty) on the Highland main line in the summer of 1959 was a leisurely business in the all-steam Far North. The Black Five ruled when it came to passenger traffic and had almost a monopoly on the route. The LMS coach on the left has seen better days as the paint is peeling off the roof. The BR maroon livery has almost superseded the red and cream standard of 1948 and passengers chat while waiting for the oncoming train. The line was opened throughout to Wick and Thurso by 1874 – that's the two road engine shed just visible beyond the bridge, by this time not long at all for the world.

The final extension up the Wear Valley took place in 1895. It had reached Stanhope as a vassal of the Stockton & Darlington Railway back in 1862 and in the years since had brought forth an enormous quantity of mineral traffic; the extension to Wearhead only came, unfortunately, once the full flush of this had gone. Working the line remained profitable for many years but by BR days traffic had declined sharply; it closed to passengers in June 1953 and the line was cut back to St Johns Chapel in 1961. The line's great strength was

limestone and this led to the establishment of a big cement works in the 1960s, at Eastgate where J39 class 0-6-0 No.64835 was shunting on a frosty day in November 1960. The engine is working wooden coal wagons of NER antecedents (joining some empties with some full ones) which were handbraked only. The decrepit station buildings at Eastgate have now been modernised and converted to a private house, and there is a project to open the line as far as Stanhope as a preserved railway.

Auchterarder station on the ex-CR main line between Perth and Stirling was closed by BR on 11 June 1956 but in this 1963 view was still intact, complete with CR signalbox and posts with standard arms. On 3 June 1963 when 5MT 4-6-0 No.44792 was working a Glasgow passenger train, the station dwelling house was still in use. No.44792 was built at Horwich in 1947 by the LMS and lasted until 1967 under BR.

Peppercorn A2 Pacific No 60528 TUDOR MINSTREL eases into Perth on 3 June 1963 with an excursion from Aberdeen. The engine was built by BR at Doncaster in February 1948 and lasted until June 1966. It appeared as No.E528 and was renumbered into the 60000 series as 60528 in 1949.

A Jumbo in Galloway 1. Ex-Caledonian Jumbo 0-6-0 No.57340 with the Whithorn goods, a three times a week pick-up, shunting at the terminus at Whithorn, 1 August 1960. The 2Fs were ideal for such light goods work. In this case it was mainly household coal from Ayrshire. The branch had lost its regular passenger traffic way back in September 1950 but freight ran until 5 October 1964. The local bus (its bright condition a striking contrast to poor old battered 57340 with its burnt smokebox door) stopped at the station at this time – a remote spot originally part of the Portpatrick & Wigtownshire Joint system. The station at Whithorn is now the local fire station.

A Jumbo in Galloway 2. 57340 at Garlieston. A grass covered platform served the occasional train which was worked on a trip basis from nearby Millisle, a distance of one mile. The line had long ago lost the excursions which it had once seen, including day trips to the Isle of Man and by now had assumed much of the character of a tramway. The official closure date is the same as the nearby Whithorn line – 5 October 1964. The weeds close in on the Jumbo on 1 August 1960; it was withdrawn from traffic soon afterwards.

A Jumbo in Galloway 3. 57340 on the thrice weekly pick-up at Wigtown, 1 August 1960. The lengthman walks along the former passenger platform to chat to the crew of the engine on the unfitted goods. He had to walk and inspect the track as prescribed in the BR rule book; bolts had to be tightened up, keys tightened and fishplates checked. The fishplates had to be oiled in the spring to allow for the summer expansion of the rails. The all bullhead rail with their wooden keys are in ancient, short, non-standard lengths, probably second-hand and brought in from elsewhere – a vintage scene of an era now utterly gone.

A Jumbo in Galloway 4. Millisle Junction on the Whithorn line, 1 August 1960, with the infrequently used Garlieston branch (notice its pre-grouping starting signal) slipping off to the right by the signalbox. The tranquil scene has been frozen in time as the signalman descends the box stairs to see the crew, the fireman standing to push the coal forward towards the footplate. The unfitted train has loaded wagons for Whithorn; once it has passed the only signs of life will be the washing flapping lazily at the back of the station building. Passenger traffic ceased on 5 October 1964.

Pretty as a picture, full of light, colour and reflection. In a view full of character 3F 0-6-0 No.57594 steams away at Redcastle station on 14 June 1960, en route for Fortrose. By 1960 the engine was based at Inverness; though Redcastle station closed to passengers on 1 October 1951 the line remained open for goods and parcels until 1960. The period piece Regional light blue notice reminds visitors that the station is still open for goods and parcels. Pink lupins flower behind the fence on the former passenger platform.

LNER shunt signals and coal spoil heaps covered in snow (reminiscent of an Arctic Circle volcano) by the former Great Central in the Nottinghamshire coalfield, through which the GCR, GNR, and MR ran and interwove in competition with each other. Coal was the foundation of the wealth of all the great companies and they fought each other bitterly for it. The Midland came first in the area, then the Great Northern and finally the Great Central. The three jostled one another through the Nottingham to Kirkby-in-Ashfield stretch, much of the output going south to feed the domestic fires of London. (T. Linfoot)

Bright, almost fairground colour signals at Truro on 15 June 1958, with 2-6-2T No.5515 dropping off the down *Cornish Riviera Express* after banking from the station. The glorious GWR signals on the approach bracket includes a shunt on the main wooden pillar. Most GWR wooden posts were replaced by tubular metal under BR, as they became due for renewal, but lower quadrant operation was retained. Truro engine shed lies on the left – now no more of course – and is crammed full of coal wagons loaded, probably, with Welsh coal. (J. Phillips)

Interior of the traditional mechanical signal box – Goudhurst on the former SER Hawkhurst branch, 6 June 1960. The line was single throughout with block posts at Horsmonden, Goudhurst and Cranbrook. The highly polished instruments were a feature of the mechanical signalling era. The tablet instrument with indicator is mounted behind the levers, some of them pulled off. The repeater is next door to the oil tilley lamp which when pumped up illuminates the cabin.

Mechanical signalboxes were sited to give the operator the maximum view of the line which was often compromised by bends, gradients or other structures, such as bridges. This is the attractive box at Gipsy Hill (a Saxby and Farmer type common on the LB&SCR as well as the SR) on 19 April 1969; it was replaced by colour light signals shortly afterwards. Some examples survive where the remaining lines on the former Region still use semaphore signalling. In this example the locking room windows have been bricked up – possibly a wartime anti-blast measure.

A relic of the former GWR on the platform at St Erth, junction for St Ives on the former Western Region. 'The cash box' was something of a railway institution, loaded into the guards brake of a train bound for the nearest town where the money would be banked. Wages flowed the other way, by similar means. A heavy iron box was used, heaved on to trains by means of a trolley and plenty of muscle power. Needless to say the WR perpetuated this GWR practice, which could still be observed into the 1970s. This was despite unfortunate robberies here and there, most memorably of the Old Oak Common wages box – more than once. The background to the Western Region nameboard (a very faded brown) is typically a semi-tropical garden of palms and lesser vegetation – a feature of many Devon and Cornwall stations. To the left is a standard GWR electric lamp fitting. (M. Wilkins)

14XX 0-4-2T No.1450 on a Sunday working (the branch milk train ran seven days a week) from Hemyock on 23 August 1964. The engine is spick and span even at this late date. Milk traffic was rated as 'express passenger' and had to be delivered immediately to keep it fresh. The branch, though closed on 9 September 1963 lasted more than another decade, until 3 November 1975 for its staple, milk. The station site was turned into a car park for the nearby creamery which operated as a margarine works until recently. 1450 was afterwards preserved by the Great Western Society.

Survivals on 26 September 1959 at Seaton in Rutland. This was junction for the Uppingham branch and an outpost of the former LNWR. The crossing gates were locked against the road, a common feature when the motor car was a rarity. The driver would have to ring that rather grand bell for the station porter to come and open up so that he could cross. In the background stands the water tower together with tubular BR signal post, and an LNWR trespass notice.

The LNWR built a line to Uppingham village to rival the nearby Midland which passed through Manton on the main line to Leicester and Nottingham. The branch, only 3¾ miles long, opened on 1 October 1884 and closed to passengers on 13 June 1960 and to freight 1 June 1964. In this September 1959 view the single LMS push and pull coach rests in the platform while the engine runs off for water. The station garden blooms in front of an LNWR ground frame and an LMS 'Hawkseye' nameboard in faded maroon. The station was conveniently situated close in the village, at that time in the county of Rutland, and presumably now in Rutland again.

Liverpool Street in steam days was a wonder to behold with locos and trains in and out constantly. East London fog often affected the station which, deep in a hollow, was smoky even in summer. The East Side station pilot was ex-GER J69 class 0-6-0T No.68619, specially painted in GER dark blue with a GER coat of arms. The engine is shunting a van on 11 February 1961 – something of the vast amount of parcels traffic conveyed by rail, even in the sixties, can be seen piled up on the left.

Steam days on the former GER line at St Margarets on the Hertford line, 24 January 1959. Overlooked by the maltings so characteristic of many GE country stations, N7 0-6-2T No.69688 wheezes past a bracket signal of lattice upright and wooden posts supporting metal upper quadrants. The train is bound for the Buntingford branch, which left the line here. One of the most picturesque on BR, it unfortunately closed to all traffic on 16 November 1964.

Hall No.5990 DORFORD HALL crosses the canal at Oxford on 13 July 1963 with the 11.6am Bournemouth to Newcastle summer Saturday train, to run via Banbury and the Great Central. The engine worked through to Woodford on the GC although Halls went to Leicester and even beyond at certain times. This location was an ever busy one, notable for the north to south trains; some changed engines, some not, but the practice was celebrated for bringing so many different classes, from four of the English Regions and – before 1948 – all Big Four companies. The end of terrace house in Abbey Road enjoyed a most singular situation...

More engine changes, at Reading on 20 July 1962. It came particularly to prominence on summer Saturdays with summer cross country traffic to the coastal resorts. The 10.42 Wolverhampton to Margate through train has changed engines and No.6998 BURTON AGNES HALL (since preserved) is in the centre with No.30915 BRIGHTON ready to take the train to Redhill where a D6500 Type 3 diesel will take over. On the left a grubby Collett 2-6-0 No.6337 is busying itself with milk vans. The Southern Region workings now come in here and the site has been occupied by electrified lines since Reading South closed on 6 September 1965.

Windermere was the elegant terminus of a short LNWR line from Kendal on the West Coast main line and was important enough to have through trains from Manchester and Euston. BR even ran a through service, 'The Lakes Express' from London in steam days. Scruffy 5MT No.45129 waits with BR Mark I coaches in the standard maroon livery on 3 August 1964. The signals are a hotch-potch of semaphores of BR origin, but on old (probably LNWR) posts.

A Black Five emerges from Linslade tunnel on 30 June 1962, shortly before electrification. The original London and Birmingham tunnel had been supplemented by additional bores but the ornate castellated portals were retained and enlarged upon. (T. Linfoot)

Holiday Interlude

Axminster on the Salisbury and Exeter section of the LSWR main line was the junction for the Axminster & Lyme Regis Light Railway of 1903. The LSWR 0415 class 4-4-2Ts were retained to work the line with its extreme curves and steep gradients. Two of the elderly 4-4-2Ts, Nos.30582 and 30584 are seen on Saturday 10 September 1960; the branch train, formed of Maunsell stock, is ready for departure to Lyme in the charge of 30582, over in the bay by the tall water tank. On such summer Saturdays BR ran through coaches from Waterloo and for the heightened service two of the class were needed. The branch survived until 29 November 1965 by which time the ancient LSWR tank engines had been superseded by diesel cars. (J. Phillips)

No.30582 has just left Cannington viaduct, an unusual structure as it was built in concrete and developed a pronounced kink owing to subsidence in the green sand and blue lias clay. The structure is still in existence today but no longer do the old 0415s plod across the valley. Of the three Adams 'Radial' tanks retained to work the branch Nos.30582 and 30584 were withdrawn in 1961. No.30583, built by Neilson on 1885, was purchased by the Bluebell Railway in July 1961 and restored to LSWR livery as No.488 – it is still occasionally steamed. (J. Phillips)

As 1960 came, the days of the individual idiosyncratic branch line, with some ancient unique survival forming the motive power, were all but up. This is Lyme Regis on 6 June 1960 with Adams 4-4-2T 30583 waiting to leave for Axminster with another all but vanished species, the mixed train. (Derek Clayton).

By 1960 lines like these seemed doomed though it had not been that long since they had been regarded as important, vital links. It was the car of course, that brought about this reverse. In 1930 the Southern had invested money in the branch, rebuilding the platforms at Lyme to much higher standards than had been enjoyed hitherto. Then, no other way of getting to the little resort could be contemplated; by 1960 the ancient roads funnelling down from the north and the east were already getting a reputation for that damnable new nuisance, the traffic jam. (Derek Clayton).

Looking out from the Lyme Regis platform end in June 1960, to the rolling woodland country beyond – hence the gradients and curves for which the line was famous, and which contributed to the longevity of the 4-4-2Ts. The little shed was built in corrugated iron, having replaced a larger wooden one which burnt down before the First World War. (Derek Clayton).

Lyme Regis in 1960, with very much of a Southern Railway air to it. The building had been reconstructed by the Southern and survived well enough to be carted off into preservation after closure of the line in 1965. (Derek Clayton).

Adams tank 30583 in the early summer of 1960, standing at Axminster. The view is towards Exeter, the main line out of view to the left with the branch curving to the right. The engine is actually on the run round loop of the bay – in the distance the branch curves left to cross the main line over a bridge. 30583 had been the 'regular' at Whitsun that year, joined at the peak by 30584 coming from Exmouth Junction. The pair, as was the practice, double headed when necessary. Later in the year track adjustments meant that Ivatt 2-6-2Ts could be tried; Barnstaple's 41297 duly appeared in September and the 4-4-2Ts were withdrawn the following year. (Derek Clayton).

English pastoral beauty, 8 June 1960, 30584 edging its way through hedge and briar. (Derek Clayton).

Southern branch line scene of a very different sort – M7 30024 in lined black runs round to platform admiration in June 1960. (Derek Clayton).

One of Top Shed's A4s, 60030 GOLDEN FLEECE at Kings Cross for departure in a typical north London 'flaming' June 1958 – a chilly, all-pervasive drizzle. The engine has just backed on and the somewhat portly driver (complete with fag) is presumably observing the actions of his fireman down on the track seeing to the coupling up. The tender is piled to the limit, the last big lumps placed one by one, by hand, at the end. (Derek Clayton)

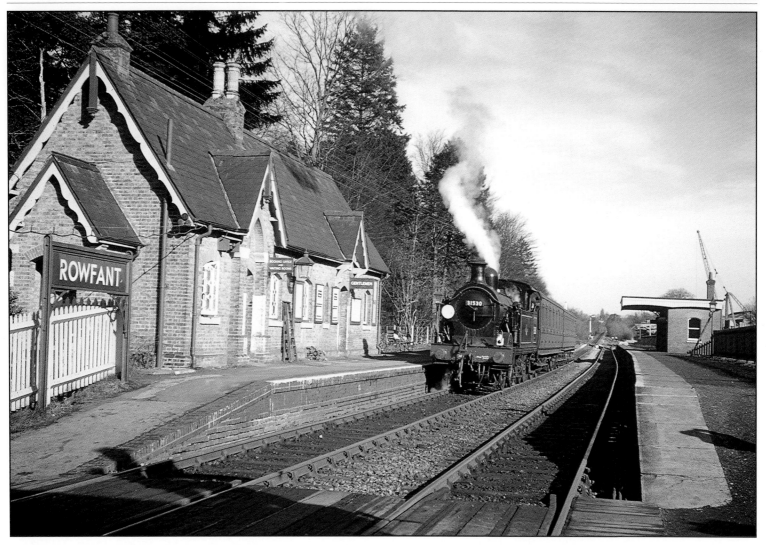

Rowfant on the East Grinstead to Three Bridges line, 21 February 1960 with an ex-SECR H class 0-4-4T No.31530, gleaming in ex-works condition. Trains were push-pull operated, using H or M7 0-4-4Ts and though the line survived the end of steam, it was closed by BR on 2 January 1967. 31530 was constructed at Ashford in July 1905, converted by the SR to motor working in June 1953 and withdrawn by BR in March 1962. The route is now a footpath and the charming station building survives in use as offices for 'Colas'.

H class 0-4-4T No.31162 pauses at Hever with a Tonbridge to Oxted railmotor on 18 April 1960. Passengers had to change at Oxted for London and travel up on the East Grinstead train. The scene is not all that changed today, except that the trains are DMUs from Uckfield to Oxted. The footbridge and station buildings survive but the service through to Tunbridge Wells ceased on 2 January 1967.

A vast Victorian engineering structure more suited to the inner parts of some great city – this was Cooks Pond Viaduct near Dormans, carrying the double track from East Grinstead to Oxted, on 7 June 1963. The lattice spans and brick piers opened with the line in March 1884. By June 1963 there was a through London to East Grinstead train every hour with a connecting railmotor to Tunbridge Wells West from Oxted. Sometimes the H class would work through from Oxted via East Grinstead as seen here – the engine working backwards with a Maunsell two coach set. The wealthy Brighton railway embarked on a series of new lines and new works towards the end of the 19th century, determined to keep the rival SER out of its territory.

The Somerset & Dorset was one of our most celebrated and dearly lamented lines, crossing as it did fine country in remote parts of these two pretty counties. Jointly owned by the LSWR and the MR and after grouping between the SR and LMS, the former looked after the buildings and the latter the trains. A hotch-potch of rolling stock and engines characterised the workings until the line's controversial demise. BR introduced the 9F 2-10-0s, which proved unexpectedly ideal – one of the Bath allocated 9Fs, No.92205, leaves Bailey Gate on 2 August 1960.